I0190208

Give It Wings And Let It Fly Away

By

Ken Maxon

Ken Maxon

Give It Wings And Let It Fly Away
By Ken Maxon

Copyright © 2014 by Ken Maxon

All rights reserved. No part of this publication may be reproduced, stored in a retrieval system, or transmitted, in any form or by any means, electronic, mechanical, photocopying, recording, or otherwise, without the prior written permission of the author except in the case of brief quotations embodied in critical articles and reviews. For further information contact ASJ Publishing at the address below. Any resemblance to real persons, living or dead, is purely coincidental.

Edited by Carol Maxon
Cover Art by Anna Jackson

ISBN: 978-0-9925982-4-2

Published 2014 by ASJ Publishing
ASJ Publishing

www.asjpublishing.com

10 9 8 7 6 5 4 3 2 1

Dedication

A special thank you to Ryta Ranf for helping me to see the world through different eyes. I had tried to write for years and finally was able to accomplish the task, not once, but twice now.

To my daughter Hope, I would like to say there is nothing in the world you can't do if you persist, learn, love and hope. Most of all, do everything with love in your heart.

To my family, Mom, Carol; Dad, Bill; my brother Jeff and sister Jessica, and the far too many friends to mention, thank you for being my support group and my sounding board for life in general.

My family, friends and readers who offer feedback as I write are the inspiration for many of the poems in this collection, I am merely the mouth piece through which it flows until you realize you can fly on your own wings...

A special thank you to my friend Rick Stephenson and my mom, Carol, for assisting with editing, catching errors, and making the job of bringing this together much faster and easier.

Especially, I would like to thank Chris and Anna Jackson at ASJ Publishing for allowing this collection and my previous collection to come to print.

To a friend, JB and her son MC. I have no idea what the future holds for either of you, but I hope you take flight and perhaps see the world as a better place. You were friends when I needed a friend.

Also, a quiet thank you to a musician taken from us far too soon, Van Stephenson. I know his brother Rick as a friend, but only recently learned of the family connection. I'm honored to consider the family among my friends. Van immortalized himself, and some of us will always remember his contributions.

Ken Maxon

Where do these thoughts come from? That is a question difficult to answer. Perhaps I've evolved somewhat over the caveman days of yore (or at least made it to the edge of the male primordial pool), or maybe I have a tortured soul who writes because of (or in spite of) that torture as therapy, or even perhaps I just have a muse that whispers in my ear to notice the beauty (or pain) of the world (or a friend) and I pay attention once in a while and jot it down...

There are a few Easter Eggs in this collection for those that care to look. At least one of the poems started as a haiku. That's the only hint I'll share at this point though; enjoy the poetry for what it is. Those that feel the need to solve mysteries will probably find the rest on their own.

Haiku

A soul for a soul
Loved unconditionally
Traded willingly

Like a gentle rain
Shedding the pain of the past
Renewing her life

Why can't we all love
Everyone on the planet
Like we're supposed to

As you go through life
The past, present and future
One day will be one

Her beauty shines through
Like moonlight on the desert
Drawing all to her

Sparkling starlight
Accentuates her beauty
As she is sleeping

To accept one's love
Gentle as a rain shower
Can be difficult

Painful choices made
Torn between past and present
Another dream lost

When I first saw you
The riddles of the cosmos
Were all solved at once

Ken Maxon

Walking together
Seeing the stars in their eyes
Hopeless romantics

The wind rustles leaves
Whispering a song of hope
For a better life

Fly high on the winds
Above the clouds with the birds
Find your destiny

Looking in your eyes
Days long ago I saw love
Now I see nothing

Seek hope where it lives
Just like faith and fantasies
It lives in the heart

She walks in shadows
Trying to go unnoticed
Yet her soul shines bright

Love, like a snowflake
Never the same pattern twice
Each is beautiful

Her spirit broken
Shattered like a broken glass
She cries in the dark

She met him and fell
Before long she realized
Oh, it's you again

Give It Wings And Let It Fly Away

Our souls were touching
For a brief moment in time
Hearts seeking shelter

Turmoil surrounds us
But dissipates if we wait
Like a morning fog

Above the turmoil
Spreading her wings to the skies
She seeks happiness

She wakes each morning
Longs to feel life's wonderment
Yet feels unfulfilled

Though the journey's long
Through sunrises and sunsets
Life continues on

Hold a woman's heart
Gently as a butterfly
It's just as fragile

The Key

The key to her heart
Is in the last place men look
It's found in his heart

Cats

As I fill your bowl
Feline eyes say your love is
Unconditional

Ken Maxon

An abused woman
Like a flower stepped upon
Is still beautiful

Silently Pondering

The sun sets on another day
The last of the rays fading away
I long to feel your touch
And miss you so much
To sit down and talk
Or go silently for a walk
Look into your eyes
Or stare at the skies
Is what I'd really like to do
But as of yet, I haven't met you

Alone

Wandering alone in the darkness
Through what she knows as life
A mixture of good times and sorrow
Some good memories, some cut like a knife

She's not always physically alone
Her life she sometimes shares
But even when there's a partner
She wonders if he truly cares

Does he push her to follow dreams
Help her up when she falls down
Emotions always cloud things
She wonders if he'll stay around

Is it really true love they feel
Or are they just killing time
Perhaps one of them is learning something
For the next step of life to prime

She's never quite certain
For most of us it's the same
Life's path is unknowable
To know the future would be a real shame

If you knew how it all ended
Some steps you wouldn't take
You might miss an experience
For fear of a heart ache

Ken Maxon

Is it just me?

Her heart how it dances
Her mind, it is free
It's always on display
For the world to see

Always she's happy
No matter the time
Everyone she meets
Agrees she's sublime

There's always a smile
Gracing her face
Setting a precedent
For the whole human race

Her life appears perfect
She's an angel in flight
But few know what she feels
In the darkness of night

The dreams of the day
Change after moon rise
The happiness most see
Is merely a disguise

It's the hopes that she has
Of what she wants life to be
Does anyone else see it
Or is it only me...

Beauty

Beauty surrounds us
Yet we let it pass by
Perhaps we're too busy
So instead we cry

We say we are looking
It just isn't there
The world is uncaring
So why should we care?

Change your perspective
Use your heart not your eyes
Your heart sees the truth
It filters out the lies.

Life

Standing in the stalls
Staring at four walls
Many people live this way
Until their dying day

Perhaps they venture
Ever so slightly more
But always with a net
Barely farther than before

Take off the string
And learn how to sing
Dance in the rain
Yourself don't restrain

Life is the journey
Not the destination
Don't be a train
That never leaves the station

Ken Maxon

Eyes

As she walks into a crowded room
Everyone else fades away
For she is more beautiful
Than anyone who has entered that day

Not just beauty on the outside
But beautiful inside as well
Surprising, for if you get to know her
She's been through the wasteland of hell

A smile that can light up a room
In her eyes are secrets untold
All I can do is helplessly watch
The never ending story unfold

In them I see
The man I'm to be
So take me by the hand, join me
I'll rescue you and you rescue me

Broken?

Broken and battered,
Shattered and torn
Longing for acceptance
Through night and through morn.

But nothing is wrong with you
You're reliving the past
Memories of old
That linger and last

In some type or form
It's baggage we all carry
Sometimes it surfaces
And can be pretty scary

It's OK to feel it
But don't let it stay
Give it some wings
And let it fly away

~Voices From The Past~

Hurt and anguish, Pain and despair
Sickness and health intertwine in the air
Many of us find life doesn't seem fair
When we see others living with nary a care

Don't give up the fight, live full every day
Never from happiness far ever stray
In each other's hearts you'll each always stay
Enjoy every moment, let your heart lead the way

Ken Maxon

More Haiku

As the sun rises
Releasing a bright new day
Make the most of it

As life progresses
As the acorn to the oak
Grow into yourself

The ache in her heart
Has for too long ruled her life
Caged like a song bird

The stars in the sky
Light the passion in her soul
Then she lights the way

The sun shines on her
Yet she sees only darkness
One day she will shine

Pain, anger, heartbreak
Memories of days gone by
Torturing her soul

As the sun rises
And dissolves away the fog
Her spirit awoke

The pain in your soul
Released on gossamer wings
Allows you to love

The wind in the trees
Softly sings a melody
Of love, happiness

Give It Wings And Let It Fly Away

Her soul is in pain
It cries out in the darkness
Does someone await

She walks silently
Traversing the universe
Forever alone

The light in her soul
Illuminates the darkness
Why can't she see it

The choices we make
Like rain on the mountaintops
Are the tears we cry

Dark and stormy nights
She gazes out the window
How did she get here

The birds sing their song
The roses and tulips bloom
Because you walk by

Once there was nothing
Then a star fell from heaven
And you landed here

As time passes by
Just as spring returns each year
A broken heart mends

You've been hurt before
Live each day to the fullest
Love with all your heart

Ken Maxon

She stares at the stars
She's remembering the past
Hopes for the future

Walking through this world
You are not truly alone
Lest you choose to be

Her strength seems to be
As strong as any oak tree
But inside she cries

Still her scent lingered
Gentle as a butterfly
He longed for her touch

The scent of the rose
Subtle yet overwhelming
Reminds me of you

Her eyes are intense
Her soul as bright as the sun
When she is in love

The mountain is high
And the journey may be long
Love is worth the cost

She reached for the stars
Fearful of what would happen
Thankful for the bliss

A love that is lost
Perhaps never meant to be
Lives on through others

Give It Wings And Let It Fly Away

Her soul wants to sing
Loudly with all of the birds
Yet she is silent

The fairy tale waits
Quietly and patiently
For you to write it

Your soul sings to me
Gentle as a summer rain
Loud as thunder

The pain that she feels
Merely smoldering embers
No longer a fire

I try to forget
Sounds you made my soul cry out
Memories linger

Finally one day
After all the tears she cried
A phoenix arose

Love fully each day
Love is a complete circle
It returns to you

The moon and the stars
And all the heavens delight
Whenever you smile

Dream of tomorrow
Then root those dreams in today
So they may Flourish

Ken Maxon

We are intertwined
Apart but never alone
Soul mates forever

Staring at the sky
She longingly wonders why
She has not found him

Love and accept love
Every person you meet
Is seeking the same

To never feel pain
Means you have never felt love
Embrace them fully

We reached out and talked
We shared a moment in time
Memories linger

The sun this morning
Crossed over the horizon
Because she arose

The stars are shining
The heavens fill with delight
Because she is happy

The heavens and stars
Give up their sparkle and shine
To glorify her

On a rainy day
She finally awakened
To see the beauty

Give It Wings And Let It Fly Away

I will shine today
As sure as the sun rises
Because you are here

She is passionate
Yet she hides it from the world
Afraid of the pain

Loyalty in love
Like the first flower in spring
Rare and beautiful

Looking in your eyes
Questions of the universe
Are softly answered

As she is sleeping
The world unfolds around her
Like a rose in bloom

Like a butterfly
She touches his hardened heart
Flying gracefully

As we pass through life
Time caresses us gently
A silent lover

She shines like the sun
Shows happiness to the world
Yet cries in the dark

Sunlight through the window
Accentuates her beauty
Adds warmth to her soul

Ken Maxon

Like a rare flower
A woman's beauty unfolds
For the world to see

Pain and fear lingers
Like a fog in the morning
Fades with the sunrise

She smiles every day
Though she feels pain in her heart
Feels lonely inside

Rising from their roots
Escaping their boyhood traits
Men sometimes evolve

Softly like the dawn
Gentle as a summer breeze
Her soul awakens

Her soul shines brightly
Everyone is drawn to her
As moths drawn to flame

She enters the room
Everyone sees her beauty
Except for herself

She awakes gently
Sheds off the pain from her past
Finds peace in her soul

The sun is rising
Bringing warmth to the flowers
Creating beauty

Give It Wings And Let It Fly Away

Her heart longs for love
Elusive as a rainbow
Solid as a rock

Life mirrors nature
Relationships follow pain
Rainbows follow rain

The love in your soul
Give it wings and let it fly
Soar with the angels

The pain in her soul
Instead of letting it heal
She holds it tightly

Softly like a dove
Quietly like an angel
She enters his life

Time flows like water
Carving its way through your soul
Creating beauty

Leave the past behind
Shed the pain like falling leaves
A new beginning
She covers the scars
Paints a smile upon her face
To hide all the pain

The love in your soul
Is a renewable source
Share it with the world

No matter the pain
You suffered through yesterday
This is a new day

Ken Maxon

Her beauty still shines
Though she has been trampled on
And survived to tell

The things that we want
Don't happen when we want them
Only when it's time

There's no stronger bond
Than a parent to a child
Or people in love

A life ends too soon
Because of a tainted love
Stop the violence

An abused woman
Like a flower stepped upon
Can still recover

Love, like a flower
Both beautiful and fragile
Handle it gently

Thunder and lightning
The touch of a gentle breeze
All when you are near

You did nothing wrong
The universe has a plan
All is forgiven

Staring longingly
Into the unknown abyss
Her eyes hold secrets

Give It Wings And Let It Fly Away

She holds back her love
Been preyed upon too often
Keeps it well hidden

Her love is boundless
But she hides it deep inside
Afraid to show it

Like the sun rising
She brought light to the darkness
An unending love

Moonlight shines on her
Lights up the stars in her eyes
Happiness abounds

Raindrops falling down
Washing away the heartache
Returning her smile

The flowers in bloom
Accentuate your beauty,
Bow as you walk by

Ken Maxon

The Fairy Tale

Alone in the darkness not seeing her own light
She says she tried but couldn't get it right
Nothing she did was ever really wrong
But anyone who entered would someday be gone

Again the sun sets on another fateless day
Thoughts of happiness keep fading away
Sleep when it comes is torture at best
The heart and the soul would love to have rest

Alone in the darkness, her heart and soul cry
The hopes, the wishes and dreams start to die
How did she fall, where did it go wrong
Why is it always a long lonesome song

To wake in the morning with an internal peace
The pain and the heartache finally to cease
With both good and bad, by life she's been bitten
But the fairy tale is sitting there, it's just waiting to be written

Feelings only fade
Perishing like the flowers
To return in spring

Her smile when I'm sad
Rainbows on a cloudy day
Her eyes say it all

The Dream

I lie awake at night
Wondering how you are
Hoping it's more
Than love from afar

Are you awake too
Are you thinking of me
Or have I become
A long lost memory?

The talks that we had
The hugs that we shared
That moment in time
That our lives briefly paired

The sun, it seemed brighter
The moon shown it too
The stars a bit clearer
Just because of you

I still lie here thinking
As night turns to day
Wondering what I did
Why you ran away

Perhaps I did nothing
And it wasn't as it seemed
Perhaps I created it all
In a single night as I dreamed

Ken Maxon

Life

Looking at her life
Full of beauty and pains
She mourns for the losses
Appreciates the gains

It's been up and down
But through it she's learned
To let go of the bad
While happiness gets yearned

Each day is new
With opportunities to spare
She can reach out and take them
Life's joy she can share

Miracles

Miracles occur
If we honestly believe
Positive thoughts
In your mind retrieve

Hope for the best
Know it will work out
Keep your heart focused
Remove all the doubt

Never lose hope
Don't succumb to the fear
For the miracle you await
Is usually quite near

Give It Wings And Let It Fly Away

Waiting in the wings
Never knowing what life holds
Or living fully

She's well connected
The heavens scream when she's hurt
Rain falls while she cries

Painted in the stars
For they who take time to look
Are all life's secrets

Take courage in life
Feel the strength of the tigress
Also be gentle

She enters the room
Her soul shines through the darkness
Brighter than the sun

Ken Maxon

The Saga Continues

I don't know where I stand
One day we flirt the next you're cold as snow
Even when we talk
I don't know where the conversation will go

The timing is always bad
It never lines up right
But to be truly honest
I don't even know if I'm in your sight

Perhaps we're only just friends
Or you're just being nice
Maybe even you're afraid
So to hide you become ice

I can't it overthink
What good would it do?
I'll just rest my thoughts
Until there's a sign from you

Just Don't Brood

Some days I wonder did I break your heart
Others I wonder if you broke mine
Then there's the question
What if we both laid it all on the line

Would we survive it
Could we stand up to the test
Would each of us bring out
In the other the best?

Or would we crumble
Give in to our fears
Succumb to what we've each been through
For far too many years

We could play it safe
And never find out
Probably the simplest route
Without a doubt

If we were to follow
That path all through life
Would we spend time wondering
Would it cut like a knife

The treasures of life
Are not found by the meek
They are the spoils
Of those who truly seek

So the question becomes
What kind of people are we
The timid or the brave
In time we shall see

Ken Maxon

Evening Fears from Both Sides

Nighttime has fallen
Most people prepare for bed
They're tired yet smiling
But she feels fear instead

When the sun goes down
Her dreams become real
Her past comes alive
Her happiness it will steal

She relives every moment
That shattered her life
Tossing and turning
Remembering the strife

As for me, I'd like to save her
Bring her back to the now
Perhaps show a better future
But alas, I don't know how

For I'm on the sidelines
Kept at arms length
To battle those demons
Would I have the strength?

Who am I kidding
To her I'll never be near
For she doesn't even know
That I am here

Give It Wings And Let It Fly Away

Haiku

She sits quietly
Contemplating decisions
It will all work out

She walks in this world
But her heart and soul exist
Among the heavens

Your life and mine
Are intertwined together
Inseparable

Watching over you
Angels need protection too
That's why I'm here.

Looking in her eyes
I see all there is to know
And I fall in love

Looking in her eyes
I see an endless future
Wonder and beauty

Ken Maxon

Ending the Lies

I've been lying to myself
For far too long
It's become a safety net
An old weary song

I say we're just friends
And convince myself it's true
If I ever were to be honest
I'm more than fond of you

I can't say anything more
Because we've never taken that chance
We'd both have to reach out
To change that circumstance

So friends we will remain
Until the timing is right
Or God in the heaven
Changes the stars in the night

Perhaps we're just living
With too many fears
Been beaten by life
And shed too many tears

Afraid to give up
What we already know
Afraid it won't work
And we'll have nothing to show

Maybe each thinks
The other won't follow
And then we'll be left out
Feeling totally hollow

Give It Wings And Let It Fly Away

Maybe one day
The stars will align
I'll become yours
And you'll become mine

Dancing

We take a step closer
Run two steps away
I wake up each morning
Which will it be today?

I'm not broken hearted
It's a funny circumstance
It's added some life
To a centuries old dance

I'm sure that sounds crazy
To read such as this
To which I'll say
There's really some bliss

For in the grand scheme
And in each retreat
The steps back become smaller
And someday we'll meet.

Ken Maxon

The Road

We stand on the edge
Of a steep jagged cliff
Perhaps we will jump
But wonder "What if?"

We could always turn back
And head down the rows
But each is aware
Of where that path goes

We've been down there once
OK, more than twice
We're used to the scenery
Some days it's nice

But then there are days
along that old trail
That we both know
We're failures on a large scale

So the question becomes
Do we sit here and wait?
Head back down the trail
Or jump and test fate?

Give It Wings And Let It Fly Away

The Story Awaits to be Finished

You reach out to me today
Ignore me tomorrow
Do I make you happy
Or do I bring you sorrow

I know your situation
Mine you know too
You're probably waiting for me
While I'm waiting for you

The future's uncertain
If we both made the change
It's not going to be better
If our lives we don't rearrange

We know what awaits us
If we keep things the same
History has shown it
But fate's not to blame

We're allowed to make choices
To make our lives better
My heart keeps saying
Go out and get her

But with each passing day
There's ne'er a clear sign
That you'd like our futures
To attempt to align

You seem to have decided
To stay where you are
So guess I'll stay here
And admire you from afar

Ken Maxon

Sometime in the future
If we're meant to be
We'll figure it all out
And set each other free

Is There More?

I see how you're treated
And yet every day
You keep on taking it
With him you stay

I know you're not perfect
For nobody is so
But it seems that you give
More than the returns show

There are people out there
Who for even a part
Would be happy to treat you well
If they only could start

You turn them away
Perhaps you're afraid
Or maybe you just think
"This is the bed I have made"

It never is easy
To sort out the one
Who truly respects you
Instead of just seeking fun

No matter what I say
I know it'll take time
To prove it's the truth
It'll be an uphill climb

Give It Wings And Let It Fly Away

But I see that you're worth it
When I look in your eyes
You deserve so much more
Than even I could ever devise

I'll give you my best
If you just say the word
For hearing you say it
Would be the sweetest song heard

Growing in the field
Flowers blowing in the breeze
Reminds me of her

Quietly she steps
Fears what life will throw at her
Afraid of true love

I see in your eyes
A flurry of emotion
Like a raging storm

Ken Maxon

Token

You smile when I'm near
But I hear you rarely smile
We talk like old friends
Who've known each other a while

I hear about the good things
And the bad things as well
Yes, it's a friendship
But there's something you're afraid to tell

I see it in your eyes
When you think I'm not aware
For I do it too
When you aren't looking I stare

I notice every movement
Every subtle stance
I try not to make you uncomfortable
Given the circumstance

You yearn for someone strong
Yet who's gentle, too
Someone who'll take the time
Getting to know and accept the real you

I'm sure you've already noticed
That I also a secret keep
No matter what I'm doing
Your memory will often creep

The linger of a touch
Or a word so softly spoken
Reminds of the past when we've talked
Of the future it's a token

Give It Wings And Let It Fly Away

Sunlight touches her
It gains as much warmth from her
As she does from it

She enters his life
Wakens something never felt
Was it just a dream?

Broken paths behind
Or an unknown trail ahead
Which one do you choose

Outside in the dark
Never finding life's purpose
A sad place to be

A gentle rain falls
Brings with it renewing strength
Erasing footprints

The smile in her eyes
Sets a thousand stars ablaze
Yet brings inner peace

Millions of stars shine
The moon will rise in the sky
Because of her smile

Nothing that I say
Will change the situation
In silence I sit

The sun sets on her
But she is not in darkness
For the moon will rise

Ken Maxon

Glistening sunlight
Dances across her features
Highlights her beauty

Rejected again
She picks up her broken heart,
Retreats from the world

Her heart is shattered
Like the waves on the shoreline
She retreats from love

Entering a room
She eclipses everything
Living poetry

I sit silently
Listening to every word
Sweet music she speaks

She weeps silently
The tears gently cleanse her soul
She is new again

She can't see herself
In the same light as others
She sees through hurt eyes

Painful memories
Have filled her soul to the brink
With no room for love

Everything changes
No matter what we desire
Just like the seasons

Give It Wings And Let It Fly Away

The gentle breezes
Blowing through the air and life
Bringing subtle change

Friendly compliments
A mistaken fantasy
Whispered on the wind

Mistaken signals
An apology whispered
No one to hear it

Sometimes one can live
A lifetime in a minute
Alone in their mind

Misunderstood smiles
A foolish man's fantasy
Strains a good friendship

Contemplative thoughts
Leading to heaven and hell
Converge both to one

A sorrowful tear
Escapes his eye unnoticed
As she walks away

A small single tear
Silently glides down his cheek
From where does it come?

Her beauty extends
Not only bound to the earth
Outshines the heavens

Ken Maxon

A moment in time
They briefly shared together
Their tears and their smiles

She smiles through the tears
Not showing the pain she feels
But I can see it

She made her point clear
The tears washed away his hopes
As she walked away

What was, what will be
Beyond imagination
Never can be seen

Sadly we all learn
The heart wants what the heart wants
No matter the cost

As she gets older
Just like a rose bud matures
Beauty in blossom

She ages gracefully
Always adding more beauty
Would I have a chance

She is above him
Much more than he could hope for
Far beyond his reach

Her grace and her poise
The softness of her beauty
Nature's perfection

Give It Wings And Let It Fly Away

She offered her heart
Asked for nothing in return
A true gift of love

True love from the heart
Is nourishment for the soul
Like rain to the rose

True love is boundless
Has no beginning or end
Like the universe

She enters the room
Her inner beauty shines bright
All motion is stopped

She flashes a smile
The planets cease their movement
Taken back in awe

Ken Maxon

The end is unknown

She offered her heart
Asked for nothing in return
But deep inside of her
For his heart she'd yearn

Long days and nights
She'd lie awake thinking
And deeper in love
She just kept on sinking

Devoting herself
With more deeper caring
Hoping their lives
One day they'd be sharing

Her own hopes and dreams
She placed on the shelf
Or perhaps it should be said
Her dreams changed for herself

The end to this tale
May someday be written
I can only hope it's a happy one
For she truly was smitten

A Song on the Wind

Whispered on the wind
Is a song of love
Gracefully flying
Like a white winged dove

Both soft and passionate
And barely heard
It's song is as sweet
As any winged bird

It gently calls out
To all who are near
But only gets heard
By a well-trained ear.

A humble existence
Can become so much more
If love washes up
Like a wave on a shore

All at once when it hits you
Like a ray of sunlight
It will fill the coldest heart
With joy and delight

Everyone it touches
Their eyes it will open
More precious is the world
For those who are chosen

Beauty is everywhere
To those that have eyes
Touched by that love
Calling down from the skies

Ken Maxon

So take care as you walk
Through this journey called life
There's plenty of distractions
Where troubles are rife

But just for a second
Force yourself to listen
For the sound of that bird
With the feathers that glisten

It might just be singing
A tune meant for you
And hopefully that day
I'll hear it, too.

Softly she whispers
A musical melody
Sets the world ablaze

She enters a room
Soft as a breeze through the trees
Making it heaven

She is, and perhaps that's enough

All the countless hours
Admiring you from afar
Wondering if you
Had fallen from a star

Your hair glistening
Your eyes shining
Reminding me that every cloud
Has a silver lining

A personality unmatched
Beauty beyond belief
Intelligence as well
What a welcome relief

Who knows what will be
The future is unknown
But my life is better
By seeing the smile you've shown

We all want to have
An unconditional love
Fulfilling our dreams

~Day by Day~

Sitting alone at twilight
My head and my heart
Are filled with memories
I wonder how did it start

It's a happy feeling
There is no sorrow
For deep down inside
I know there's tomorrow

Ken Maxon

What will be will be
I've heard it said
So as the sun sets
I keep looking ahead

To the sunrise tomorrow
Or perhaps the next week
To the time in the future
We'll again get to speak

A smile I carry
In my heart, on my face
As the future becomes now
And the journey I trace

No matter the outcome
I'm a better man now
And I still keep progressing
Because of a vow

That I would evolve
Somehow, some way
To better myself
Day after day

Just for your friendship
I'll put up the fight
For knowing you exist
Makes life look more bright

Thank you for the memories
Of the past and to come
They've given me a place
To start my life from

Give It Wings And Let It Fly Away

~Walk With Me~

Her hair glistens like moon light on the ocean
Her voice is sweeter than a singing bird
Just having her around and knowing she cares
Is the greatest love song that's ever been heard

When she isn't around life seems mundane
I wonder how I was happy in the past
Cause she's given my life a new meaning
I've finally found what my heart wants at last

I know what I'm supposed to be now
And the path to get there is finally clear
It isn't just my path to walk alone though
Please take my hand and accompany me, my dear

~The Question Answered That Wasn't Asked~

I can't explain why I think of you
But you're on my mind often
It could be your eyes or your smile
The way you make my hardened heart soften

Perhaps it's the way you open up to me
And talk about things that are on your mind
When you just have to vent to someone
And you don't think any answers you'll find

Perhaps it's the way we go for long times
When we don't have the time to talk
Then out of the blue you just show up
And we fall into that same old comfortable walk

Whatever it is that brought you to me
Be it fate, or God, or a gift from a falling star
I'm merely grateful that you're here
And most importantly you are who you are

Ken Maxon

~The Scars~

The mist in her eyes
From a lingering past
Just wanting to put it
Behind her at last

Sometimes the mistakes
Were the same ones again
Others it was new mistakes
That caused the pain then

But each time it happened
She learned a bit more
It made her much stronger
Than she had been before

Her life isn't as bad
As she thinks it to be
I can see things in her
That she doesn't see

Like a beautiful soul
That lights up the night
A deep caring tenderness
That can bring such delight

What she sees as wounds
Or deep sunken scars
Just makes her more precious
Than all heaven's stars

Give It Wings And Let It Fly Away

Could they be only
Merely fleeting memories
Or reality

A gentle caress
Like a breeze on a warm night
Makes me feel alive

~We Met~

It started so easy I never saw it coming
You were merely a friend when we first started talking
But somehow it happened that as things progressed
I noticed the same path it seemed we were walking

I'm probably creating it alone in my mind
And there will never be a chance for anything more
But no matter how hard I try to do it
I can't go back to the man I was before

You've made me become a better person
I know that wasn't your original intention
But something inside of me just clicked
I realized my life finally had some direction

Thank you for entering my life when you did
Even though it was by chance that we met
No matter what happens in the time that will come
I see life hasn't given up on me quite yet

Ken Maxon

~A New Day~

The sun is wakening
It's a fresh new day
I hear birds singing
I understand what they say

It's a day full of joy
I must grab it fast
Let go of the pain
And memories from the past

I've lived in that past
For way too long
Today is the day
To heed the bird's song

I bump into her
A meeting of total chance
Her eyes come alive

~It Began with a Smile~

Just seeing her smile
Will brighten my day
No matter what troubles me
The worries will fade away

There's something about her
The way she makes me care
Though I try not to do it
When she's around I can't help but stare

The fire in her eyes
The glow of her skin
When she walked into my life
I knew my future would begin

~Eternity~

When you walked into the room
I couldn't help but notice you
Everyone else seemed to fade away
But did you notice me, too?

The lighting seemed different
Like a scene change in a play
A spot light focused on you
I was in awe, didn't know what to say

Your eyes had a sparkle
From a deep burning fire
Getting to know the real you
Became my deepest desire

Getting to know everything
Could consume an eternity
But I would commit to that task
And recreate myself in that infinity

Light through the window
Illuminates her features
Angelic beauty

Ken Maxon

~A Normal Day~

Morning arrives
Sunlight shines through
I find my mind wandering
Thinking of you

Do you greet the sunrise
In the same way
Thinking of me
As you start your day?

The daily routines
That we all go through
Working and chores
Still I'm thinking of you

The sun fades away
The moon and stars come out
I realize quietly
You've been on my mind throughout

I lie down to sleep
The day finally I finish
And even as I dream
Those thoughts of you never diminish

For me it's a normal day
A single thought that never ends
I always smile thinking of you
Because through it all, we're friends

Give It Wings And Let It Fly Away

~Today~

This morning I rise
It's a brand new day
Will I take the chance
For what's on my mind to say?

Coffee comes first
Then for work, get ready
There's email to check
The routine is pretty steady

There're things to do
So I put if off
I don't say anything
But at myself I scoff

The day keeps on going
The time I'll surely find
There will be plenty of chances
To say what's on my mind

Evening rolls around
There're errands and dinner
The day's almost over
The time left getting thinner

Finally it's bedtime
The day is complete
I'd love to say something
But I have to get off my feet

Another day is over
Where the time went there's no clue
I missed another opportunity
To say I'm thinking about you

Ken Maxon

Another morning
His thoughts like a heavy fog
Still thinking of her

Meeting that person
Heaven and hell fade away
Soul mates forever

~Starting Today~

Lessons learned the past
Lead to a better tomorrow
If we start today
To let go of the sorrow

Yesterday has receded
Faded away into time
To let go of the pain
Isn't a crime

Remember the good things
Keep them in your soul
Let them become part of you
To enjoy through life's stroll

The future is as bright
As you let it become
Starting with today
To happiness succumb

~The Gentle Voice~

Gently on the wind
I hear a voice calling
So softly and faint
Yet I feel my heart falling

A beautiful sound
As ever I've heard
Yet so quiet it is
It seems to be absurd

The whisper I hear
Calls not from the past
Nor from the present
Or even the future at last

It's hard to explain
But it comes from all three
It speaks of what was
What is and will be

It calls me to follow
The path of my heart
There is no better time
Than right now to start

Years I spent learning
And fumbling around
But each step I stumbled
Brought me to more solid ground

I don't know the future
Or what it entails
But that silent whisper
Can show me the trails

Ken Maxon

There's still more to learn
I don't know it all
But from this moment on
I'll follow that call

She enters his life
Quietly and unnoticed
Like a summer breeze

~Meeting For The First Time?~

They bumped into each other
By a shear twist of fate
He remembered the time
He remembered the date

She came out of nowhere
Just walked in the room
Suddenly a light
Cut through his gloom

Was it the first time they'd met
Or had it been before
In another past lifetime
On a far distant shore

Standing there smiling
She washed my troubles away
Like a springtime rain

A tear in her eye
Yet a smile shown to the world
Hides the pain inside

~That Day~

The day that I met you
My view on life shifted
I realized until then
Through the past I had just drifted

I'd seen many things
And accomplished a few
But I'd never met anyone
Who was anything like you

Most people were blank faces
In a never ending crowd
But your eyes when I saw them
Seemed to be screaming out loud

You shone through the darkness
Of a life I would merely survive
And offered me a chance
To finally feel truly alive

The meaning of life and love
I still don't understand
But perhaps one day I will
If you'll just take my hand

I'll share in the joy
Face the sorrow too
It'll all be worth it
Just to share it with you

A rose in the rain
Like a woman throughout life
Is still beautiful

Ken Maxon

~**Beauty**~

The flowers in springtime
The colors of a rainbow
The singing of the birds
Or the first fallen snow

Paintings in a museum
Children in a playground
A well-tuned instrument
Making a beautiful sound

The waves on the ocean
The stillness of a mountain
Water gently flowing
In a brook or a fountain

The stars on a clear night
And a rose spotted with fresh dew
But they pale in comparison
To the beauty I see in you

~Lingering Memories~

Late at night
After the sun has set
I remember those thoughts
I've tried to forget

Memories that linger
Of when we used to talk
Stay up at night
Or take a long walk

It shouldn't have ended
I don't know why it did
But those lingering memories
Into my thoughts slid

Perhaps it was timing
We never had a fight
Neither of us ever
Gave the other a slight

Before I lay down
To get some sleep
I say a prayer
To God your soul to keep

First thing in the morning
You're still on my mind
I hope that the day
Will treat you kind

As the day goes on
You occupy my thought
I wonder if happiness
You finally have caught

Ken Maxon

I hope that you smile
That way you always do
I hope someone compliments you
The way I used to

You deserve all the best
That life has to give
I hold you no malice
As your life you live

Just know that inside
I think of you often
You were the one
Who made my heart soften

Perhaps in the future
We'll finally get it right
The stars will line up
The heavens will shine a light

No matter the outcome
I still call you friend
And I'll continue to care for you
Right through to the end

~6 Senses~

Your scent still lingers
In the cool morning air
I still feel your touch
Even though you're not there

I still see your face
Glowing in the moonlight
With every vivid detail
Forever etched in my sight

Your taste still lingers
Ever softly on my tongue
My ears still hear the music
That together we've sung

Even more deeply
Than the five senses control
I sense your existence
Combined with my soul

~An Angel on Earth~

Smiling through the pain
Laughing through the tears
Working so hard
To show courage through the fears

The past had some good times
But also it's share of bad
Many of the happy memories
Are tempered with sad

Ken Maxon

So many wounds
So many scars
Far too many nights
Alone under the stars

All of those experiences
Reaching out from the past
Have created a path
And make sense at last

They fade into the sunset
As you enter my world
The mysteries of the universe
Are finally unfurled

The sunlight seems warmer
The flowers more full
Just knowing you're there
My heart feels the pull

I understand love songs
That never made sense
Even though I put it up
You climbed over the fence

Your life has touched me
In ways I can't tell
All I can think
Is from heaven you fell

You gave up your wings
To be here with me
One of heaven's angels
On earth to set me free

Give It Wings And Let It Fly Away

~Friends~

When we first met
We were both in the rain
So we shared a few laughs
And shared each other's pain

Through the ups and downs
We've stood by each other's side
I like to think we both
Benefit from the ride

I know the deepest sorrows
We probably both contain
Neither of us wanting
The friendship bonds to strain

We've never had any contact
Except for an occasional hug
But throughout all the talking
Your presence I cannot shrug

You've touched my soul in ways
That no one has ever done
Like the deepest pit of the ocean
Getting a glimmer of the sun

Your friendship I truly treasure
It puts my mind at rest
To merely say I'm grateful
Would be inadequate at best

I'm learning words aren't always
Available to explain
The thoughts that come up randomly
Inside my feeble brain

Ken Maxon

Perhaps sometime in the future
I'll find a better way
To say what your friendship means to me
How just knowing you makes my day

~The Story is Unfinished~

There's a story unwritten
About you and me
Of what's in the past
And of what is to be

We started as friends
As always the right way
Whenever we're together
There's plenty to say

We talk about everything
That's happened to us
From all of the big things
To each little fuss

I learn from your strengths
From all you've been through
Each day I hope
I can be more like you

No matter what happens
You've always got a smile
Even though I can tell
You're hurting all the while

But you greet each new day
With a wide open heart
I see how it helps
As a fresh way to start

Give It Wings And Let It Fly Away

I watch all your movements
I study your eyes
And each time I see you
There's a brand new surprise

I see something new
That I haven't seen before
I look forward each day
To learning a bit more

I can't guess the future
Nor would I want to try
Because I'd go through it anyway
Filled with a laugh or a cry

I can't tell you the story
So don't be upset
As I said in the beginning
The story hasn't been written yet

Ken Maxon

~In Your Eyes~

Looking in your eyes
I see the universe unfold
The secrets of time
And the stories untold

It all makes sense now
After all these years
Why I had trials
And so many tears

If I wouldn't have faced them
I wouldn't have grown
Or traveled to this path
To me you have shown

The man I am now
On a journey just begun
Stepping from darkness
Out into the sun

I see in your eyes
The journey is long
But with you by my side
I know we'll be strong

Your eyes tell a story
Only known by some
They tell of the man
That I will become

Give It Wings And Let It Fly Away

~Everything~

Everything about you
Brings a smile to my face
The pain of the past
Has disappeared without a trace

The sparkle in your eyes
The light on your hair
Although I try not to
I can't help but stare

The music in your voice
When you talk about your day
I hope we still talk like this
When we're both old and gray

You say you're demanding
And difficult to deal with
But I've never seen it
It must be a myth

I haven't seen anything
That causes me grief
To be really honest
Your presence is a relief

The stress melts away
Whenever you're near
There's only one thing
That causes me fear

That someday you'll see yourself
In the same light I see
And that day you'll realize
There's far better than me

Ken Maxon

But even that knowledge
Won't stop me from caring
I wouldn't trade anything
For the moments we're sharing

Everything I learn
Makes me want to know more
I look forward to each day
For what the future has in store

Sunlight on her hair
The sparks I see in her eyes
Makes me long for her

Give It Wings And Let It Fly Away

~Friendship~

When we both met
It was a life winter season
I don't believe in coincidences
So there must be a reason

We've talked about everything
And nothing at all
We've always kept the pace
At barely a crawl

You say I'm attractive
And tell me I'm sweet
The way that you look at me
Sweeps me off my feet

You're like heaven on earth
An angel evicted
Perhaps sent here to teach me
To love unrestricted

Together it seems
We'd fit like a glove
But perhaps it is merely
An unrequited love

But friendships are love
In their own unique ways
So perhaps it will blossom
Into something more one of these days

Only God knows
What a future day brings
So for now I'll be content
An angel lost her wings

Ken Maxon

The way that she walks
With every movement she makes
She IS poetry

Poetry exists
So the world, full of wonders
Can be more enjoyed

Silently I sit
In awe of her existence
Moved by her presence

Love is a flower
That is not always perfect
Admire its beauty

You are my first thought
My ongoing fantasy
My reason to be

Contemplating life
All the unanswered questions
Until she arrived

Inside of her soul
If you care enough to search
Is the key to life

A woman's beauty
Is polished by her journey,
What she has become

A woman's beauty
Like a stone in the water
Polished over time

Give It Wings And Let It Fly Away

The wings of her soul
As she lets go of her past
Finally find flight

She fell from heaven
An angel who clipped her wings
To walk by his side

Dance to the music
Created inside your heart
And let the world watch

Ken Maxon

~Forever Lost Not Wanting to be Found~

I could get lost
Staring in those eyes
And forever be happy
I'd won the greatest prize

When it comes to music
You'd be my first choice
I could listen for hours
To the melody of your voice

The touch of your hand
Makes my heart quiver
The smile on your face
Causes me to shiver

There's nothing I would change
You're perfect as you are
I'm glad no one else
Has noticed it so far

I'll be forever lost
Not wanting to be found
Content in the knowledge
That you are around

Wishes and prayers
Sometimes come through
I did both for years
And finally I met you

~Hard to Find the Words~

Anything that I say
I'm sure you've heard before
Spoken by someone else
On a long forgotten shore

You've heard about your beauty
And the sparkle in your eyes
To hear it all again
Must surely sound like lies

I cannot find the words
To make it sound sincere
So I fumble to do my best
And struggle through the fear

It's all the little things
Your weaknesses and your strengths
And the ways you try to hide them
You go to such great lengths

I see your outward happiness
The inner struggles too
I try to notice everything
That makes you oh so you

You might ask why I bother
What makes you so great
I'll go out on a limb
And give it to you straight

Every time I see you
I notice something more
Something else about you
I never noticed before

Ken Maxon

And for each bit I learn
My heart grows all the fonder
Even when you're not around
To you my thoughts will wander

I thought I'd seen it all
Before you came along
I'd almost lost all hope
On ever hearing that song

No one stuck around
No matter what I tried
And each time it ended
Another part of me died

But everything I've learned
All that I've been through
Was merely to prepare me
For the day that I met you

Give It Wings And Let It Fly Away

~Blessings~

The way that she carries herself
Shows the world she is proud
But deep down inside
Her heart screams out loud

She longs for the day
When things turn out right
For now it seems to be
Out of reach, out of sight

Looking a bit closer
Her life's not that bad
There've been many joys
Many smiles she's had

Family and friends
And memories galore
Each day is a new day
With wonders in store

The scent of a flower
The touch of the breeze
The light of the dawn
As it touches the trees

The song of a bird
Gently caressing her ear
With God watching over her
She has nothing to fear

The feel of the rain
As it brushes her cheek
The love of her children
Her life's not so bleak

Ken Maxon

A warmth fills her heart
As her soul stands up tall
She knows that her friends
Won't let her fall

As her soul touched his
Gently as a summer breeze
He succumbed to love

As their hearts combined
She gave his life new meaning
A shared existence

~Struggles~

Some days she wakes up
And can't fake a smile
Most days are good
Some more like a trial

Mistakes of the past
Creep up late at night
Consuming her soul
No happiness in sight

The shadows remind her
Of what she did wrong
Although she tries to fight them
Sometimes they're too strong

Just when it seems
That all hope is lost
She'll walk through the gauntlet
No matter the cost

For she's a survivor
A victim no longer
The struggles she faces
Just help make her stronger

She wipes off a tear
Of happiness and sorrow
It's the start of the beginning
Of a brighter tomorrow

Ken Maxon

~Something~

Fate must have caused
Their very first meeting
Nothing else could explain
That electrified greeting

Hours spent talking
To each as a friend
Building up something
That will never truly end

She will forever be
(He'll never forget)
Always just as beautiful
As when they first met

~A Secret Shared~

The secrets to life
And all it entails
I've found as I traveled
Down life's dusty trails

I don't know them all
There's no way that I could
But I learn more each day
As everyone should

Although there are many
Too many to name
I'll pass on a few
It'll help all the same

Wake up each morning
And say a quick prayer
Be thankful for everything
That falls in your stare

Offer a smile
To everyone you meet
Let all your worries
Take a back seat

Be kind to animals
And children too
The way you treat others
Is a reflection of you

As you go through the day
Be thankful some more
Of everything around you
The beauty galore

Ken Maxon

The more that you give
The more you receive
What you send out
Is what you retrieve

The truth about life
Only known by a few
Is you get blessed by blessing
Others around you

The secret I speak of
Of course it is love
It's everywhere around you
Flowing down from above

I've just scratched the surface
But it gives you a start
On the journey through life
Just follow your heart

~Time~

Forever in my heart
Always on my mind
A wash of deep emotions
I thought I'd never find

You took me by surprise
When you wandered in that day
You added shades of color
To a life that felt quite gray

The more I get to know you
As we talk and share
I try to find the words
To tell you that I care

Give It Wings And Let It Fly Away

Perhaps there are no words
To express the feelings right
It's not enough to hear it
You'd rather know by sight

I'm sure you've heard it all before
It's the same for me as well
The best investment is time
For only time will tell

Whenever you talk
I eagerly listen
Hanging on each word
As your eyes brightly glisten

I file it in memory
I know that someday
Those things that you tell me
Will be useful in some way

I know there will be storms
We'll both have to weather
We can survive them
If we face them together

I'd much rather show you
Than just say a word
That was spoken before
By now sounds absurd

I'll put forth the effort
Claim time as a friend
And show you each day
I'll care till the end

Ken Maxon

~A Dream~

A candy bar or soda
Brings out your smile
Even when things have bothered you
For so long a while

Life knocks you down
And I say a silent prayer
Hoping a blessing
With you God will share

You ask for so little
Yet deserve so much more
You're a wonderful person
Right down to the core

I know I'm not worthy
But each night I pray
That I become a better person
With each passing day

Perhaps it will work
And the stars will line up right
To be more than a dream
To kiss you good night

~Mornings~

In the morning when I wake
And get out of bed
I go through the motions
To clear the cobwebs from my head

I plan what needs done
Make a list I've been taught
Then I think of you
A calming, quiet thought

The chaos around me
The busy daily grind
Fades to the background
As you fill my mind

Each little chore
That I do every day
I hope makes life easier
For you in some way

To really be honest
To say what is true
My most important priority
Every morning is you

Ken Maxon

~Respect~

Silently crying
Alone late at night
So tired of daily
Putting up a fight

The lack of respect
That was hard fought and earned
Apparently was just
Another life lesson learned

When does it stop
Where will it end
How does one find
For once a true friend

Maybe tomorrow
Or some future day
The path will be clearer
A light shining the way

Some days existence
With struggles are a must
A few tears get shed
In a prayer placing trust

Give It Wings And Let It Fly Away

~<u>Start Today</u>~

Today's a new day
To make a fresh start
To follow your dreams
And follow your heart

Putting it off
Because the timing's not right
Will only keep your dreams
Just out of sight

The mind over thinks
The heart will not lie
Take that first step
Go ahead, give it a try

The only true failure
Is not taking the chance
Sitting on the sidelines
Never making a stance

When I see her smile
Her existence is heaven
Shining down on me

She sits there smiling
Beautiful as a flower
Shining like the sun

Like a butterfly
She gently touches his heart
Adds color and life

Ken Maxon

~Just Because~

What do I see
When I look in your eyes
The world I have known
Sheds away it's disguise

I see in your eyes
A world filled with hope
A quiet mountain stream
Flowing down a flowery slope

I see in those eyes
A storm in a rage
An animal that's wild
Long confined in a cage

I see a bright future
Built from rubble of the past
The broken hearts and trials
Make sense at last

Your eyes tell a story
I hope never ends
For both of us it started
Long before we were friends

The secrets of the universe
Are answered there too
Questions I never thought to ask
Until the day I met you

When I look in your eyes
Each time I see more
I look forward each time
To see what's next in store

Give It Wings And Let It Fly Away

~Someday Soon~

Another life chapter
It seems to be near
As always it's filled
With some happiness and a tear

The book is not finished
Only a few pages
But the storyline it seems
Has been going on for ages

The characters all change
But the plot is the same
The scenery is different
But always the same game

It is what it is
I've heard someone say
So I keep striving on
Looking forward to the day

That I meet the right one
In the right time and place
Who'll spend life beside me
With a smile on her face

I'm not really old yet
But there're more days behind
Than I have yet in front of me
For that love to find

I'll just keep on going
At life do my best
With a hope in my heart
And let a prayer do the rest

Ken Maxon

I know that you're out there
You're looking too
Hopefully it will be soon
That I'll finally meet you

Who am I kidding
We've already met
But apparently it's not
The right time for us yet

As she walks along
Not knowing where it will lead
The stars guide her path

She is not perfect
But when she entered my heart
She fit perfectly

Give It Wings And Let It Fly Away

~Bright as a Star~

I hear your sweet voice
Whispering in my mind
A dream that's been fulfilled
One I never thought I'd find

No matter where I look
I see your face at every turn
I long for more than the memory
To see you again is what I yearn

The smile that highlights your features
It always seems to be there
A shining outward expression
That says you truly care

I can't find a fault in you
No matter how hard I look
Somehow that empty space in my heart
The pain I felt, away from me you took

You teach me a bit more
About happiness each passing day
I'd like to return that favor
Perhaps one day I'll figure out a way

There's so much I want to tell you
Show you how great you really are
You don't seem to see it yourself
That you shine as bright as a star

Ken Maxon

~Another Day~

Another day begins
Which will it be today
Full of bright colors
Or endless shades of gray?

Does it really matter
In the grand scheme of things?
For each day is full
Of many beautiful things

A black and white photograph
Shows off as many details
And brings out more subtleties
That the picture entails

Look for the beauty
Search with your heart
For each day you wake up
Is a new path to start

Give It Wings And Let It Fly Away

~God's Creation~

I see you a bit differently
Than you see yourself
You seem to place your dreams
High upon a shelf

You think you're a mess
With all you've been through
But I see something different
Every time I look at you

You always seem happy
Shining as bright as a star
But under the surface
You seem afraid to reach out too far

Perhaps you're afraid
You don't deserve it today
Or that if you receive it
It'll be taken away

Maybe life has beaten you
Before so many times
That you actually feel
You committed some crimes

Whatever the case
I can tell you it's lies
I see something differently
When I gaze in your eyes

You tell me the bad things
You think you have done
To tell you the truth
It sounds more like fun

Ken Maxon

I see an angel
In heavenly dress
I don't know this person
You think is a mess

I see perfection
Created by God's hands
The most beautiful person
Anywhere in these lands

Someone exquisite
Both inside and out
You may not see it
But to me, there's no doubt

~Life's Artwork~

If a poem was a painting
It would look like you
Perfect in every way
Showing colors anew

If a song were a feeling
It would be your gentle touch
As I'm consumed by your hug
That could never happen too much

If a picture were music
It would sound like your voice
No matter the other options
It would be my first choice

I live a whole lifetime
Each time we're together
Be it a few moments
Or a blessed forever

~Dreams~

Her smile lights the way
Through a world full of shadows
Blazing a new trail
Leading where, only God knows

The light in her soul
Shows clearly the way
I see my destiny unfolding
The place where I long to stay

As she gently takes my hand
This is where it will all start
I feel the relief from past worries
As from my memories they slowly depart

This is what I've strived for
What I'd hoped to be shown
But the depths it entails
I could never have known

Throughout my whole life
And the dreams I could see
The reality you created is better
Than the fantasy could ever be

Ken Maxon

~Nature Knows~

Sunlight shines
On her glistening hair
A bird on a branch
Catches her in it's stare

A soft rain falls down
To wash away her tears
The moon and the stars
Offer protection from her fears

A rose blossoms
Because of her smile
So she can be carefree
If only for a while

A gentle breeze
Caresses her cheek
Even nature knows
She is the one to seek

~Worthiness~

When we first met
You fit like a glove
But now I'm beginning to accept
It's just an unrequited love

We've had great conversations
That have lasted for hours
We've been through the sunshine
And survived the showers

I've heard the stories
That pop into your head
And listened to the times
About the tears that you've shed

You say you're a mess
From all you've been through
But to be really honest
I've never met anyone as perfect as you

You have a great personality
And a never ending smile
Your eyes shine like the stars
Captivating me all the while

I've spent most of my life
Not lonely, but single and alone
Figuring out what I did wrong
Trying to find ways to atone

Making up for mistakes
I've made in the past
To meet someone like you
And be worthy of it at last

Ken Maxon

I doubt I'll ever be more to you
Than just a simple friend
But if you let me be there
I'll stay till the end

Give It Wings And Let It Fly Away

~Love and Life's Other Subtleties~

I was about to give up
Thinking I had made too many mistakes
To ever meet someone like you
Who gives more than she takes
To know we'll never be together
My heart, it truly breaks

I tried to get to know you
I really gave it my best
I don't know when it happened
But I obviously failed the test
So I'll pack away my feelings
As best I can and give you a rest

If sometime in the future
Your feelings should change
You don't have to put yourself on a limb
I'd never want to make you feel strange
But find a way to say it subtly
And my life I'll rearrange

Ken Maxon

~A Mask~

Sometimes I wonder
As I look in your eyes
Are you really happy
Or is it just a disguise

Behind that bright smile
Are you covering up pains
Using it as a shield
As your soul slowly wanes

Then I have to wonder
Why you go it alone
What could you possibly have done
That you would have to atone

None of us is perfect
We all have a past
The trick is to forgive ourselves
So we can move on at last

Give It Wings And Let It Fly Away

~Tomorrow~

She lives a life full of love
Looking happy all the while
No matter what is happening
She always shares a smile

Surrounded by friends all the time
And a family that helps and cares
She seems to have all she could want
More than most in their hopes and prayers

She's attractive and friendly
Beautiful both inside and out
Anyone would be honored
Just to be near her, no doubt

Onlookers can't see past the surface
Things aren't always as they seem
Her life isn't a fairy tale
It's not the seemingly perfect dream

Hiding behind the smiles and joy
Is a life full of pain and sorrow
Remembering and reliving the past
Hoping for a better tomorrow

Ken Maxon

A gentle caress
A touch from heaven above
She touches my heart

She is everything
The rain, the flowers, the sun
Moon and stars in one

She is the sunrise
The very essence of love
Bringing life anew

Recently they met
The pieces fell into place
It was meant to be

Perfectly they fit
Two lost souls on the same path
A two piece puzzle

~If That's The Worst, I Can Handle It~

She is perfection
Even though she doesn't agree
If there is anything wrong with her
It's something I can't seem to see

She'll say it's because of her health
Or something her kids think
Or that she's hard to deal with,
Will push people to the brink

She can name a hundred reasons
Probably think a thousand more
But when it comes to reality
They're excuses and nothing more

She perhaps is trying to justify
What's happened in the past
Perhaps it's so she can push away
The memories she's amassed

Perhaps it's much more subtle
After all that she's been through
She doesn't think she deserves it
That happiness is for the few

But again she is perfection
Standing before my eyes
She'll never convince me differently
No matter how hard she tries

We all have our list of issues
It makes us who we are
For as we've traveled down the road
Life has taken us far

Ken Maxon

It's a never ending journey
With no beginning and no end
Why would we spend it all alone
It's better traveled with a friend

I can handle all the bad
You mention when we talk
For I know the best is yet to come
As down life's road we walk

~Someday~

If e'er you get tired
Of going it alone
And want someone in your life
To finally call your own

Someone who'll share with you
Both good times and bad
Revel in the happiness
Offer a shoulder when you're sad

Always see your beauty
No matter how you feel
Always give in easily
When a kiss you try to steal

When the storm is raging on
I'd share with you an umbrella
I may not be a prince
But you are my Cinderella

If you need to hear it
I'll sing your favorite song
To see that you sleep well at night
When the day has been too long

Give It Wings And Let It Fly Away

No matter what life throws at us
I'll be there by your side
Through all the ups and downs
Of life's ever changing tide

I know it won't be easy
Nothing worth it ever is
But each of us has strengths
To cover the weaknesses

For though you don't believe it
Every word is true
I knew you were my destiny
When I laid eyes on you

Maybe one day, someday
When we're both old and gray
You'll finally come to realize
I'm really here to stay
I won't ever leave you
And I mean each word I say

Ken Maxon

~A New Day~

Life has its moments
Both good and bad
I try to spend my time
Remembering the fun I have had

Some days it's harder
To put on a smile
When life throws out curves
Every foot walked feels like a mile

All of the worries
The continuous daily grind
Everywhere I turn
More stress is what I find

Then I take a breath
Close and open my eyes
Slowly on the horizon
I see the sun starting to rise

The moon and the stars
As they fade from the view
I also take a moment
Just to think about you

The flowers in bloom
The dew on the grass
The peaceful serenity
On the water like glass

The sun hits the trees
The birds take to flight
The last song of the whippoorwill
As it sings it's goodnight

Give It Wings And Let It Fly Away

The peace and the calm
Makes my soul yearn
I'm surrounded by beauty
Everywhere I turn

It's a beautiful day
With another new start
It warms me inside
Love fills my heart

I know that you're out there
And someday we'll meet
Secure in that knowledge
The new day I'll greet

When she is near me
I feel her presence, her warmth
A ray of sunshine

I feel her presence
Gently like a summer rain
Caressing my soul

Ken Maxon

~Another Day~

Another good cry
Won't solve anything at all
So I'll put on a smile
And pretend to walk tall

It's become the routine
Filling day after day
I think about daydreams
Letting my mind go astray

The fantasies are better
Than the truth that surrounds me
At least in my head
I can be truly free

Someday in the future
Perhaps with some luck
Things will be better
Than where the present seems stuck

Give It Wings And Let It Fly Away

~The End?~

This collection it seems
Is still incomplete
There's so much to say
But for now I'll retreat

Perhaps another time
Or perhaps another place
I'll write once again
With style and with grace

But for now it must end
And draw to a close
When the muse will return
Only God himself knows

Who else knows the future?
It's certainly not I
But I'll now close this chapter
A sad tear in my eye

I'll pray things work out
For the best as they should
For you truly deserve happiness
You deserve someone good

It's no longer appropriate
So I'll lay down my quill
No matter what happens
I'll think of you still

Your memory will linger
In both heart and mind
It's someone like you
I'm still hoping to find

Ken Maxon

I won't dare complain
I found a good friend
Or at least that's what I'll say
Until my life's end

Perhaps in this journey
There's something to be learned
As another chapter is finished
And another page gets turned

ABOUT THE AUTHOR

Ken has been a professional broadcaster, newscaster, production director, operations manager and voice over artist since 1988, hosted an 80s retro show, morning talk show, afternoon drive classic country show as well as several other formats and shifts.

He's a proud father of a teenage daughter who thinks his job is *"really cool"* and her name reflects his view on life- "Hope".

Ken resides in the mountains of rural central Pennsylvania in the middle of nowhere with about a dozen cats that call him *"meow"*.

He hopes that you have enjoyed reading these as much as he did writing them.

www.ingramcontent.com/pod-product-compliance
Lightning Source LLC
Chambersburg PA
CBHW061753020426
42331CB00006B/1458

9 780099 259824 2